THE
QUEEN

First English edition published by Colour Library Books Ltd.
© 1983 Illustrations: Keystone Press Agency, London.
© 1983 Text: Colour Library Books Ltd., Guildford, Surrey, England.
This edition published by Greenwich House, a division of Arlington
House Inc., distributed by Crown Publishers, Inc.
h g f e d c b a
Display and text filmsetting by Acesetters Ltd., Richmond, Surrey, England.
Printed and bound in Barcelona, Spain. by Cayfosa and Eurobinder.
All rights reserved
ISBN 0 517 429780

THE QUEEN

PRODUCED BY
TED SMART & DAVID GIBBON

GREENWICH HOUSE

The Queen

Queen Elizabeth II is a serene and dignified monarch, the Royal Sovereign of the British Crown. She rules by the rights of a constitution that is over eleven centuries old. In fact, the monarchy is the oldest secular institution in Britain, dating back to the year 829. The Queen traces her descent from this time, when the Saxon King Egbert of Wessex united the whole of England under his leadership. The monarchy is many centuries older than Parliament and founded the British judicial system. Its continuity was once interrupted, however, by Oliver Cromwell, who governed Britain for eleven years from 1649 to 1660.

It was at the end of the seventeenth century that Parliament established a monarchy with only limited rights. Before this, the kings and queens of this land personally exercised supreme executive, judicial and legislative powers. By the end of the nineteenth century, the political power of the sovereign had been vastly reduced and the Queen now has to be an impartial head of State, and must accede to the wishes of Parliament. She remains by right the ruler of the country, under a number of Acts, by common law rules of descent and, more importantly, by the wishes of her loyal subjects. The Queen is undoubtedly one of the best-loved monarchs in the entire history of the British Crown.

When she was born, it was never considered that Elizabeth would succeed to the throne, but it was her destiny to do so. Her father was the Duke of York, the second son of King George V. However, her uncle Edward VIII (later the Duke of Windsor), abdicated in her father's favour on December 11, 1936, broadcasting to the nation: "I have found it impossible to carry the heavy burden of responsibility and to discharge my duties as King as I would wish to do without the help and support of the woman I love", referring, of course, to Wallis Simpson. Now the young princess "Lilibet", at the age of ten, was heir presumptive. She was trained as a future sovereign, and was educated privately, concentrating on languages, history and music.

In early 1939, Elizabeth and her sister, Margaret, went with their father to visit Dartmouth Royal Naval College. Here she was impressed by the nephew of Earl Mountbatten, Philip, who acted as the royal escort. He was eighteen at the time, five years older than Elizabeth, and had just started his training at Dartmouth. He graduated before the start of the Second World War and went to sea as a second lieutenant. Two years later, he was mentioned in despatches while serving on the battleship HMS Valiant, which was in action against the Italian fleet off Cape Matapan. His Captain later said: "Thanks to his alertness and appreciation of the situation we were able to sink in five minutes two eight-inch gun Italian cruisers". Meanwhile, Elizabeth was suffering alongside her future subjects the rigours of wartime England, and toured with her parents the bomb-ravaged areas of the country. When she was old enough, she joined the army as an officer in the Auxiliary Territorial Service, forerunner of the Women's Royal Army Corps, though there was opposition from her family and the government. She was trained in motor transport driving and maintenance, early demonstrating that, as today, a Queen can "walk with Kings..." and not "...lose the common touch".

During the war, Philip continued to meet Elizabeth at Windsor Castle, and the young princess fell in love with the dashing naval officer. Her parents, however, were not too keen on her choice, feeling that she needed more time to meet other eligible suitors. Philip was born a member of the Danish and Greek royal families; his mother was Princess Alice of Battenberg and his father Prince Andrew of Greece. He obtained naturalisation papers two years after the war, becoming a British subject, and a few days later the King told his ecstatic daughter that she could marry her beloved. The engagement was announced on 9th July, 1947, and the wedding took place in Westminster Abbey on 20th November of the same year, the day after George VI had created her fiance' Duke of Edinburgh. Her father was to write to her, after the wedding: "I can see that you are sublimely happy with Philip." He also wrote to her on honeymoon what was a lovely, simple letter to a daughter: "I am so glad you wrote and told Mummy that you think the long wait before your engagement and the long time before the wedding, was for the best. I was rather afraid that you had thought I was being hard-hearted about it...Our family, us four, the 'Royal Family' must remain together, with additions of course at suitable moments! I have watched you grow up all these years with pride under the skilful direction of Mummy, who as you know is the most marvellous person in the world in my eyes, and I can, I know, always count on you, and now Philip, to help us in our work. Your leaving us has left a great blank in our lives but do remember that your old home is still yours and do come back to it as much and as often as possible."

Prince Philip personally decided to devote himself to the promotion of British industry and exports. He also introduced the Duke of Edinburgh Award Scheme, which has been so instrumental in the encouragement of youngsters to participate in a variety of activities, including adventure sports and community projects. He is also a principal champion of Britain and the Commonwealth, giving support to its nations whenever required.

Their first child, Prince Charles, Duke of Cornwall, was born on 14th November, 1948. He was to be followed by Princess Anne (born 15th August, 1950), Prince Andrew (born 19th February, 1960), and Prince Edward (born 10th March, 1964).

In 1951, Princess Elizabeth began to represent her father, King George VI, on various state occasions. His health was failing, and Elizabeth, as the next monarch, had to begin preparing for her future duties. Philip, as her consort, was given "extended leave" from his role as skipper of the frigate HMS Magpie – even today, he still remains in that status officially, although he is now an Admiral of the Fleet! In February 1952, Elizabeth and Philip were in Kenya on the first stage of a royal tour of East Africa, Australia and New Zealand, when news was brought to them that the King had died.

With the death of King George VI, the cry from town hall steps throughout the Commonwealth was "Long live the Queen". A new Elizabethan Age had commenced. The Queen was met on her return to England by her Prime Minister – Winston Churchill. When she next saw her mother, it was the Queen Mother who would bow to the new Sovereign and, as protocol demanded, would bravely make a speech to her daughter's subjects: "Your concern for me has upheld me in my sorrow and how proud you have made me by your wonderful tributes to my dear husband, a great and noble King. No man had a deeper sense than he of duty and of service, and no man was more full of compassion for his fellow men. He loved you all, every one of you, most truly. That, you know, was what he always tried to tell you in his yearly message at Christmas; that was the pledge he took at the sacred moment of his Coronation 15 years ago. Now I am left alone, to do what I can to honour that pledge without him." On 2nd June, 1953, the young Elizabeth was crowned in Westminster Abbey. A hundred thousand people lined the streets to see their Queen. Although she was now sovereign head of the greatest group of nations in the world, her reign would see the gradual dissolution of the British Empire, as independence was granted to many countries under the Imperial sway. She is, without doubt, one of the most significant figures of the twentieth century, still Queen of a vast Commonwealth of Nations, bound together by common ties of history, justice, harmony, tolerance, friendship and tradition.

Politically, the Queen has "the right to be consulted, the right to encourage and the right to warn" (Walter Bagehot). She has regular weekly meetings with the Prime Minister to discuss the affairs of Parliament and, of course, her signature is required on all Acts of Parliament before they become law. She has been on many more tours abroad than any previous monarch and the influence she has throughout the world cannot be calculated. She is one of the best ambassadors for this country, and paves the way in cordial foreign relations and trade. The Civil List, from which she pays all her staff, is small next to the benefits accruing from the ties of friendship between nations; although her reign has, thus far, been full of global conflict. Unfortunately, 1982 was to see war in the Falklands, with the "soldiers of the Queen" as well as her own son – helicopter pilot, Andrew – going to fight once more for this nation, echoing the occasion, almost four hundred years before, when her namesake Elizabeth I addressed her troops: "I know I have the body of a weak and feeble woman, but I have the heart and stomach of a king, and of a king of England too; and think foul scorn that...any...should dare to invade the borders of my realm."

Her Majesty has a very great interest in horse-riding, and especially in the breeding and racing of horses. It is said that on the eve of her coronation, a lady-in-waiting said to her: "You must be feeling apprehensive Ma'am", and the Queen is reputed to have replied: "Yes, but I'm sure my horse will still win". A few days later, Aureole came second in the Derby. The Queen's other famous favourite animals are the corgis. She has about ten, all of which are descended from one called Susan, who was even taken along on the royal honeymoon. If the Queen is at one of the royal homes, she will ensure that she is free at about 4 p.m. so that she can feed her dogs, among which are black labradors, with a mixture of meat, gravy and dog biscuits, served with a silver fork and spoon!

Her daughter, Anne, is a tireless worker for the Riding for the Disabled Association and the Save The Children Fund, of which she is president. An excellent equestrian, she was courted by Captain Mark Philips, who was a member of the British team that had won gold medals at the Munich Olympics in 1972, where Anne was a spectator. In November 1973, they were married in Westminster Abbey. She was driven there in a glass coach with her father, with cheering crowds all the way. The coach had been used by her mother and father on their wedding day, and the tiara she wore had also been used by the Queen.

At the time of her silver wedding anniversary, the Queen indicated how important family life is to her: "A marriage begins by joining man and wife together, but this relationship between two people, however deep at the time, needs to develop and mature with the passing years. For that it must be held firm in the web of the family relationships, between parents and children, between grandparents and grandchildren, between cousins, aunts and uncles. If I am asked today what I think about family life after 25 years of marriage I can answer with simplicity and conviction. I am for it."

1977 was Silver Jubilee Year, and seldom can there have been more spontaneous demonstrations of the love and loyalty in which she is held by her subjects. It was a year that demonstrated the busy public life of the Queen. On February 14th, she went to the Kingdom of Tonga, then on to Fiji. By the end of the month she was in New Zealand and in early March, Australia. This was followed by a visit to Papua New Guinea. She returned home to tour Scotland, England, Wales, and Northern Ireland by August. The Queen also, on the 6th June, lit a special Jubilee bonfire in Windsor Great Park, which signalled a chain of similar bonfires being lit all over the country, to commence the celebrations. In her Jubilee Luncheon speech at the Guildhall in London, she said: "When I was 21, I pledged my life to the service of our people and I asked for God's help to make good that vow. Although that vow was made 'in my salad days when I was green in judgement' I do not regret nor retract one word of it!" Elizabeth II is truly a dedicated monarch, much admired and loved.

29th July, 1981, saw her son and heir, Charles, married to the lovely young Lady Diana Spencer. It was a glorious, fairy-tale wedding, full of sumptuous pageantry. It also showed once more, the world-wide appeal of the affairs of royalty.

In the difficult times in which we live, the courage of the Queen was shown in the Mall on 12th June, 1981, when a series of blank shots were fired at her by a teenager. She managed to control her startled horse and prevent it from bolting, and the youth was overpowered by spectators and police.

"Uneasy lies the head that wears a crown", and the Queen, acting in the full glare of publicity, is often put under pressure by the media. But outwardly, she is calm, sometimes seeming slightly aloof. Some of the press reports are considered "amusing light reading" – the colourful, weekly Paris newspaper *France Dimanche*, is regularly sent to Buckingham Palace for this reason, by the British Embassy. It has reported the Queen's abdication at least seventy times, and has contained over eighty reports of her intention to divorce Prince Philip!

Her sons are all fine young men. Charles, the 'Royal Adventurer', is one of the best-loved members of the Royal Family. He is known for being rather sensitive and thoughful, with a delightful sense of humour. Many people have speculated as to whether the Queen would abdicate in favour of her son, and not keep him as an heir-in-waiting, as the future Edward VII had been kept by Queen Victoria. But, there is little evidence that she will. In South Africa on her twenty-first birthday she said that she would dedicate, "my whole life, whether it be long or short...to your service". Then, during a major speech of the Jubilee, referring to that first speech, she reaffirmed that promise. However, Charles is content in his present position, living his life under his personal standard, emblazoned with the words: '*Ich Dien*' – I Serve. His brother, Andrew, is an accomplished helicopter pilot serving with the Royal Navy, in the family tradition. Sometimes he hits the headlines for his amorous exploits, but he is a likeable personality. Recently, Edward, the youngest brother, has said that he wants to join the Royal Marines when he has finished at university. No finer training could be had for the vigorous life of a royal, than with these commandos!

The Queen

The Sunday Times once published the results of a poll, in which people had been asked why they thought the monarchy was important. The percentage results were revealing:

Helps keep the Commonwealth united	69 per cent
Adds colour to people's lives	66 per cent
Makes violent revolution less likely	64 per cent
Sets standards of morality	61 per cent
Prevents political parties becoming too powerful	58 per cent
Sets standards of manners and dress	52 per cent

The Queen has managed to fulfil these many roles with grace and panache.

Today, the Queen and her family are more popular than ever. She is unmistakeably royal, head of a glorious institution – the British Crown. Why is the constitutional monarchy so popular? Walter Bagehot claimed that: "Royalty is a government in which the attention of the nation is concentrated on one person doing interesting actions. A republic is a government in which that attention is divided between many, who are all doing uninteresting actions. Accordingly, so long as the human heart is strong and the human reason weak, Royalty will be strong because it appeals to diffused feeling, and Republics weak because they appeal to the understanding." He also claimed that, "The best reason why Monarchy is a strong government is, that it is an intelligible government. The mass of mankind understand it, and they hardly anywhere in the world understand any other."

One of the constitutional functions of the Queen is the State Opening of Parliament. It is on this occasion that she reads out a statement outlining her government's intentions for the following year. The key point is that it is "Her Majesty's Government". The ceremony follows a procession from Buckingham Palace to Westminster, where she sits before the robed Peers in the House of Lords. It is a tradition going back to William the Conqueror, whose custom it was to tell his barons, earls and bishops exactly what he expected them to do in the immediate future.

The Queen believes in the role Great Britain can still play in the world, and possesses a strong sense of leadership. Her Majesty knows the way she would like to see her land: "Over the centuries perhaps the greatest moments in the history of our country have been in times of great adversity when the nation has stood alone, when we have been faced by the threat of more powerful material forces, but have been sustained by the strength of our own moral and spiritual conviction. Under God's will, we can still achieve that truer greatness in our own generation. For it is part of the Christian message that 'time and chance happeneth to all men.' Opportunity lies with each and every generation in the circumstances of its day provided it acts with faith, courage and perseverance."

Her Majesty at the ceremony of Trooping the Colour (previous page). She has attended all the major royal weddings of her reign. Her sister, Margaret, was married in May 1960 (above); her daughter, Anne, in November 1973 (opposite, top) and her son, Charles, in July 1981 (opposite, bottom). Her own wedding portraits, from November 1947, are shown (top and right).

The Queen has reigned over Great Britain and Northern Ireland since 1952. Her vitality and enjoyment of her royal duties is obvious (both pages). During the time that she has been Sovereign, she has witnessed enormous changes: the British Empire is no more; only the Commonwealth remains.

In October 1981, during a visit to Dunedin, New Zealand (right), the Queen was given a photograph of the Royal Family from July 1947, taken at the time of her engagement to Prince Philip. It is now customary for her to meet her subjects in such informal walkabouts.

Her Majesty has to attend numerous public engagements and is admirably supported by her husband, Prince Philip. She has managed to maintain a happy and contented family life despite the constant pressures of affairs of state. Wherever she goes there are crowds of well-wishers (above), showing their continued support for the monarchy.

With the Duke of Edinburgh, Her Majesty has travelled all over the Commonwealth. She is greeted as Queen by her subjects throughout the world. However, she and her husband had to part from each other (below) after a visit to Canada in April 1982. Philip gave her a swift but unprecedented public kiss at the bottom of the aircraft steps. In March, they were hosts to Sultan Qaboos of Oman (bottom). Close relations with Oman go back to the 1970s, when the Sultan was aided by British soldiers, who later helped defend his country against guerilla incursions.

The roles that the Queen undertakes are numerous. She attends the State Opening of Parliament each year (top left), seen here with Charles and Anne in November 1973, travelling in the Irish State Coach. In May 1982, she went to Westminster Abbey to install new Knights Grand Cross of the Order of the Bath (top right). Inspecting the Coldstream Guards (centre left); the Queen attending the Royal British Legion's Festival of Remembrance (above); visiting the Chelsea Pensioners (left and far left) and inspecting a detachment of the Yeomen of the Guard (right).

The Queen has travelled more extensively than any previous monarch. Although she is often surrounded by cameras, Her Majesty is also a keen photographer herself. On all her royal tours she takes a camera with her and loses no opportunity to add another picture to her private collection. However, the gloomy weather at the 1976 Montreal Olympics (top left), forced her to keep the camera case shut on more than one occasion! The Queen uses a variety of cameras, as seen on these pages, and her interest is of course echoed by other royals, notably the Earl of Lichfield and Lord Snowdon.

The Queen is honoured by her subjects in all her lands. Garlands of flowers are given to her to show love and loyalty. When she visited Tuvalu, in October 1982, the people brought her to the island in a canoe, then carried her ashore on their shoulders (above). Later, she was crowned with frangipani flowers (right). Canada and Sri Lanka (opposite top) also gave floral tributes.

Diplomacy involves her in meeting many international figures. The Queen of the Netherlands' State Visit in 1974 (above left); Holland in 1958 (right); Her Majesty arriving for the State banquet given by King Khalid of Saudi Arabia in June 1981 (bottom left); hosting Commonwealth Prime Ministers at Buckingham Palace in 1977 (bottom centre); at a dinner given by the Canadian Prime Minister, Mr Trudeau (bottom right) and at a banquet during the same tour to the Canadian provinces in 1978 (opposite). Arriving at the Pipers' Ball (top right).

The Queen's visit to Tuvalu (opposite pages) in 1982, was a mixture of warmth and informality. The canoes in which she and her husband arrived, were built of a light hardwood called puka, and cost no more than £150. They were copies of those used locally for skipjack fishing, brightly painted for the occasion.

Prince Philip is arguably the most travelled man in the world, averaging 75,000 miles a year. He attends many engagements with his wife (this page) but now limits himself to some 250 – 300 a year. However, he did once travel 1,500 miles to squeeze in 30 different functions and make 15 speeches in the course of a single week.

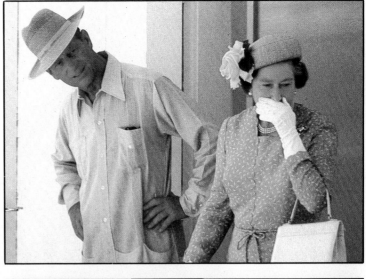

In April 1982, the Queen and Prince Philip were in Canada and attended several official engagements as part of the handing over of the country's constitution. She welcomed guests to a State reception and banquet in Ottawa (right and top left). She was wearing a matching combination of diamond and ruby jewellery – the tiara was made up from her own collection of stones for the visit to Windsor by the President of Mexico in 1973. The Queen had previously been in Canada in 1978 and is pictured wearing a Canadian Order on her evening dress (above). In December 1982, Her Majesty attended a new production of *Peter Pan* in support of Great Ormond Street Hospital (top right). At a medal-awarding ceremony in Australia (opposite page).

The Queen is pictured at her desk at Balmoral in the summer of 1972 (top left). Only rarely do she and her husband use Balmoral Castle other than for their summer holiday, but in January 1977 they had photographs taken which were published on the 25th anniversary of her accession to the Throne (left and top right). On her 30th anniversary in 1982, they were at Sandringham (above and opposite page, top right). The Queen is very interested in the racing and breeding of horses and attends many equestrian events (opposite page). In thirty years she has not yet achieved her avowed aim, "to breed a horse that wins the Derby".

The role of monarch involves much pomp and ceremony. The balcony at Buckingham Palace has held many a royal group as shown on these pages. In June 1982, she and the rest of the Royal Family (opposite page, bottom left) witnessed and acknowledged the Royal Air Force's birthday tribute to the head of the armed forces. In this role, the Queen leads her troops on horseback on her Birthday Parade. The 1981 ceremony of Trooping the Colour was marred by an incident in the Mall when six blank shots were fired at her. She quickly recovered her composure and was all smiles on the balcony afterwards (opposite page, second from bottom).

The Queen arrived in Bahrein on a tour of the Gulf States in February 1979. She entertained the Amir on board *Britannia* (opposite). On the Saudi-Arabian visit she was greeted by King Khalid at Riyadh airport (above) and conferred with him (below). In 1982, she was host to the Sultan of Oman (below right).

Elizabeth II, gracious Sovereign Queen, is Britain's finest ambassador. Following in the wake of her many travels, trade and foreign relations improve and the esteem held for this country abroad, grows.

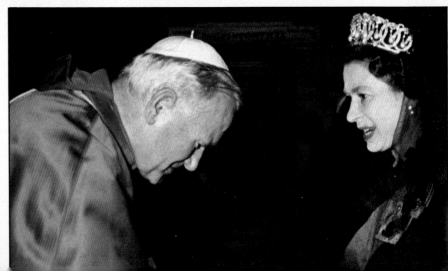

A forty-minute meeting took place on 28th May, 1982, between Pope John Paul II and the Queen (previous page – Her Majesty dressed in blue). This followed an audience with the Pope in 1980 (remaining photographs).

On these pages can be seen members of the oldest Order of Chivalry in the Kingdom: The Most Noble Order of the Garter was founded in 1348 by King Edward III and is now celebrated each St George's Day in Windsor Castle.

During 1982 the Queen had a special word for 99-year-old Dorothy Kennish in Brisbane (top). She meets some monks in Sri Lanka (above) and the families of RAF personnel (left). Opposite page: the Queen admits that she is, not particularly renowned for her green fingers, but is seen at the Chelsea Flower Show (top left) each year.

When she went to Merseyside in May 1982 (centre left), there was one group of protesters waving banners proclaiming "Reality not Royalty" and chanting slogans. Others tore down the banners and began singing the National Anthem. There was quite a fracas but the Queen, with practised aplomb, appeared not to notice.

There has always been a special relationship between Britain and the United States. The first President to stay at Windsor was Ronald Reagan, who went for a canter with the Queen in Home Park (opposite page, top left). Ever ready with a wave and a smile, Her Majesty wins the affection of millions. In Australia, she met the French singer Sacha Distel (above).

In May 1982, she followed the fortunes of her husband in the International Carriage Driving Grand Prix (top right). In June of the same year, she inspected the RAF Regiment (right) and was also seen at a Commonwealth variety performance in Brisbane (bottom left) and at the Commonwealth Games in October 1982 (bottom right).

At Kandy, Sri Lanka (opposite), ceremonial umbrellas accompanied the Queen and Prince Philip. She also visited Tarawa (above) where she received honours in the form of dried-leaf garlands and plaited cords. While in Canberra she visited the War Memorial, after which the crowds (right) were waiting to meet her. At Windsor Castle with President Reagan (top right). The Stallion Show, Newmarket (below).

The Reagans celebrated their 31st wedding anniversary on 4th March, 1983, when the Queen held a dinner on board *Britannia* in their honour (opposite page, top left). The previous June they had visited England, arriving at Windsor to be greeted with the rousing strains of the British and American national anthems. Protocol demanded that the Queen and President Reagan should stand level with each other. At the last moment, however, Mrs Reagan stepped forward, leaving Prince Philip and Prince Charles behind (opposite page, bottom right). President Giscard d'Estaing of France visited the Queen in 1977 (right). In Qatar (top right) inspecting a guard of honour, one of her many duties as a visiting monarch.

The Queen and Queen Mother are pictured together at the 1981 Derby (above). While her mother is keen on steeplechasing, the Queen is interested in flat racing. In earlier days they jointly owned a chaser, but Her Majesty gave up her interest when the horse broke a leg and had to be destroyed. At Royal Ascot (top left, top right and centre left). She gestures expressively while talking with Princess Michael (left) at the Derby. On the morning of one of the four days of Ascot, the Royal Family have use of the course for their own private race! Prince Philip is, of course, more interested in four-in-hand carriage driving; Princess Anne likes three day eventing and Prince Charles has a penchant for polo, riding for the Maple Leaf team and Les Diables Bleus, although the press has a field-day photographing him whenever he falls off his horse.

A montage of pictures of the Queen, fulfilling her many roles (previous pages). The Trooping of the Colour (these pages) is a custom going back many years. The flag itself would be carried among the soldiers on the eve of a battle so that they could recognise it as a rallying point amid the battle's smoke and slaughter. Ceremonially parading the colours of a guards battalion – embroidered with battle honours – before the sovereign, began in 1805 and has continued each year since. The Queen has made a point, throughout her reign, of leading her troops as Commander-in-Chief of the armed forces, off the parade ground and along The Mall. She rides side-saddle on a police horse that has been trained to behave placidly amid all the din of the military bands and the cheering and shouting. 1,600 officers and men from five regiments of foot-guards and two regiments of horse-guards take part.

Queen Elizabeth II heads perhaps the most stable monarchy in the world. As head of a vast Commonwealth of nations, she is uniquely placed to propound the virtues of democracy, freedom and the pursuit of individual liberty. In these days of social unrest, the durability of the Royal Family is a force for traditional values.

At the Coronation of Queen Elizabeth II in 1953 it rained. When she visited the Reagans in California there were floods and she had to spend a night in a hotel. No wonder she takes an umbrella with her!

Manchester in May 1982 (above); in July 1982 it was Scotland (below); California in March 1983 (right). Indeed, when she went to Kiribati in the South Sea Islands, a man was hired to ensure good weather.

Above all, the Queen is the head of a family in which children play a very important part. Now with the birth of Prince William (opposite page, top), Her Majesty has three grandchildren.

Opposite page: the Queen visits Merseyside (top left); Reading (top centre); Perth (top right); Adelaide Country Club (bottom left); Perth (bottom centre); at the annual parade of the Chelsea Pensioners (bottom right).

This page: on the tour of Australia and New Zealand (left); on a visit to Canada (bottom left) and to Brisbane (below), where she collected so many bunches of flowers that journalists following her had to help carry them!

In California as guest of the Reagans (previous pages). The Queen is the head of a monarchy that is the oldest secular institution in Britain. She traces her lineage back to Cerdic, who landed here in 495. Her Majesty is the head of the Royal Family; this country's constitutional monarch; head of the Church of England and of the Commonwealth, so fulfilling many roles both as Sovereign and mother.